Bestest!
Thank you for
lifelong support
no matter how far.
I love you♥
xo Jaeyun

VIBRANT EVOLUTION: The Beauty in Becoming

A Workbook Collection of Letters and Poems

JASMYN RUJA

This book is for you and dedicated to anything that allows you to heal, love and be free from fear. The road isn't always easy, but we can always find beauty in it.
This is my art.

TABLE OF CONTENTS

I.	THE IMPORTANCE OF MENTAL HEALTH: AN OPEN LETTER	6
II.	THE PURPOSE	12
III.	A LETTER OF ENCOURAGEMENT	17
IV.	A LETTER ABOUT FEAR	19
V.	A LETTER ABOUT PAIN	23
VI.	EXPERIENCING THE PAIN	26
VII.	THE EVOLUTION	29
VIII.	"I CAN DEFINE MYSELF"	31
IX.	THE UNDERSTANDING	42
X.	A LETTER ABOUT PEACE	44
XI.	EXTENDING FORGIVENESS	47
XII.	A LETTER ABOUT RESTORATION	48
XIII.	NOTE TO SELF	51

THE IMPORTANCE OF MENTAL HEALTH: AN OPEN LETTER

Suicide accounts for the loss of more than 41,000 American lives each year, more than double the number of lives lost due to homicide

*In the year 2015, 2,504 African Americans (AA) died by suicide in the United States. Of those, 2,023 were men and 481 were women.

Yes,
AA people suffer from mental illnesses
AA people have suicidal thoughts,
And AA people have been killing themselves.
Break the stigma.

Suicide Hotline: 1-800-273-8255

*This information can be found on the American Association of Suicidology's official website at suicidology.org

Mental health and mental wellness is important to not only learn about, but to talk about in the African American community. We need to begin creating spaces where these kinds of issues can be addressed in a safe environment. We have a culture of making it appear like we have it all together because we don't want to show signs of weakness, but this mindset is what's killing so many of us.

We've been trained by learned behaviors to keep everything under wraps, and God forbid we ever openly discuss our failures, feelings, or anger. We aren't allowed to cry because we don't have anything to cry about. We cannot show anger unless we want to fit the stereotype of the angry black woman or the violent black man. We can't be upset with our life's circumstances because somebody else has it worse somewhere in the world. We're constantly told how we should be feeling. We should be grateful that we have a life to live, a house to sleep in, and food to eat. We should be thankful that we have clothes on our backs. We should be grateful that we have "freedom", but are we really free in mental bondage? Where were we taught how to reverse the effects of the generational pains of slavery? When were we taught that we are human beings and human beings are allowed to feel and express emotions? We've only been taught how to survive, but now it's time for us to learn how to heal.

Mental illnesses are categorized under a large range of mental health conditions that affect your mood, thinking and behavior. The exact cause of mental illness is not known. There are combinations of various forces that have an effect on mental health. Sometimes mental illness can be passed down from your parents, or there could be a defect in the processing of neurotransmitters in the brain. Certain environments, drug abuse, childhood trauma, domestic violence and poverty can contribute to mental health issues as well. There are a lot of different factors that come into play in what causes one to experience mental illnesses, so researchers have a difficult time giving it a single known cause, but, therapy and counseling are always options.

They have different kinds of therapies for different things, and it's not as intimidating as it may seem. If someone wants to focus on changing a specific lifestyle habit they could select behavioral therapy with a behavioral specialist. If they want to discuss certain topics and become more self-aware they might choose cognitive-behavioral therapy, which is the most widely used form of therapy (the one we see in movies). This form of therapy is a psychotherapy that aims to change specific dysfunctions in our thinking, emotions and behaviors (with emphasis on the way we think). It's the one where you sit in a comfy chair and talk about your problems to someone who assists you in digging deeper within yourself.

And if you're reading this thinking, I don't want people to be able to have access to the evidence that I'm going to therapy, you're in luck. All of the information that you discuss in therapy is confidential. Your records are confidential, your appointments are confidential, and your progress is confidential. So, you don't need to worry about any of your information getting out because it's illegal for therapists to disclose information discussed in therapy unless you give them permission to do so. It's actually pretty fun too, once you get over the fact that you're talking to a complete stranger. Therapists have a way of pulling things out of you without you even noticing, so just think of it as learning about yourself with assistance.

Being vulnerable is something that I have never been too fond of. I was never 100% comfortable with people knowing everything about me. The idea of people knowing too much about me was something that I had no interest in being a part of. I didn't care to share personal, or emotional experiences with anyone (friends, family, in relationships, etc.). In my head, I had this idea that if I didn't share things with people, it would protect me. I believe that most people have felt this way at some point in our lives, and I can't help but question where we get this idea from. Where do we get the idea that it is shameful to share experiences, or if we show emotions we are somehow weak? I believe in liberation through expression. I believe that we are able to heal by speaking about the things that we go through. I believe that others can be healed through our own courage to speak up.

When I started going to therapy, I was in my early college years on a journey to find out who I was. I genuinely wanted to go into a space and have someone pull information out of me, and they did. It was uncomfortable at first because, like I mentioned earlier, I didn't want my therapist or anyone to know too much. The first time I ever went was awkward, I didn't really say much because I was feeling my therapist out. She asked a lot of intake questions, just to get a general idea of who I was and of my goals in therapy. Then, she told me to tell her about myself... My initial thoughts were *"Tell you about me? Girl, what? Aren't you the therapist? You tell me about me"* because that's how I expected it to work, but of course it didn't.

    I started telling her small surface things, like how old I was, what school I went to, what I was studying, etc., just to see how good she really was. Then, as I'm talking about surface things, I found myself getting deeper: *"My parents are divorced"*, *"I have two older brothers, I'm the youngest"*, *"I've always felt super connected to people"*, *"I feel like I was born to be different"* and I realize what I'm saying, and I think *"oh, she's gooooooood. Get me to dive into myself head first, eh?"*, and that was just the first session. Every time I went back I learned something different about myself. It's such an empowering experience because it gives you a place to heal yourself and assistance when you don't know where to start.

    Ever since I started going to therapy, I knew it was a part of my purpose to share the positive impacts of therapy and help break the stigma within our community. Mental Health is something that I hold so close my heart because I've been in so many instances where people around me were not ok but didn't know what to do about it. I can even recall times when I wasn't ok and didn't know what to do about it. I've been around people with so much pain inside of them and they've always been drawn to me for help. I've been in so many instances where I've had to talk people off of the ledge, some of them I didn't even know, and I have always been confused as to why I always knew exactly what to say to make someone second guess their suicidal thoughts. It's never made sense to me how the words that need to be heard just come out of my mouth.

    I say all of this to say, I know God has placed things inside of me that can move people into internal healing, and for a long time I've been afraid to use the gifts God has placed inside of me. But, this book is my own my declaration of independence from being a slave to my mind, my biggest act of courage and self-liberation. This book is my freedom letter to my past self.

As I write and release my art into the world, I am declaring that my liberation begins with my decision to live confidently in my truth, and my decision to walk courageously in my journey. My liberation begins when I decide that no one can take my story and make me who they want me to be, because I am a woman who is exactly who she wants to be – constantly growing and consistently creating. My freedom begins when I relinquish the fear that keeps me hidden from the world, because I am here to make an impact, and I declare that I will be all that I am destined to be.

To you, I pray that my words will help you find healing, strength and love within yourself. I pray that this book will begin to heal families, friendships and relationships. I pray that this book will begin to heal and move you away from any mentalities and blocks in your spirit that are keeping you from success and happiness. I pray that you will begin to understand the purpose of your life, and the gifts that you have inside of yourself. And I pray that this book will allow you to continue to grow into the person you're meant to be with confidence, patience and determination. I pray that this book can be your liberation, and you can take what I used as a freedom letter to set yourself free.

xo, jas

THE PURPOSE

Proverbs 18:16 (NIV): A gift opens the way and ushers the giver into the presence of the great.

The accidents happened during a time where I was struggling to come back to a place of closeness with God. I was struggling with my identity, with my healing, and with my purpose. I wasn't as engaged as I should have been in my classes, I was trying to find a church that felt like home, my focus wasn't on God. I just felt lost. I was trying to figure out what my gift was and how I could use it to help people, but it felt like I was just moving through life for no reason. God had blessed me with overly supportive and encouraging people in my life that would always push me and encourage me, but during this time I felt stuck.

Now, there were three accidents – my best friend and I involved in all three of them together. The first one was in September of 2016. It just us two in the car, but it was the accident that triggered something inside of me that was telling me that I wasn't good enough. It's like a switch went off inside of me. I had constant thoughts that were telling me that it wouldn't get any better, and I believed them. My self-talk was negative, and I was not understanding how powerful my words were. I went through a period of extreme anxiety to everything. I was questioning everything, good and bad, I was upset because I had put a burden on my parents and on my friends, I had no clue how this was going to be worked out, so I felt hopeless. I continued through life trying to push these things to the back of my mind, and it worked for a short period of time but not for long.

    The second accident was in October 2016, with one of my other friends, with my best friend also in the car. It was homecoming week, and we were running last minute errands to get us ready for the evening when we made a left turn and a Chevrolet Silverado style truck (the ones with the flatbed) rushed through the yellow light and made an impact in the passenger side where I was sitting. As a result, my best friend, who was sitting behind me, and I were seriously injured. The car made a direct impact with my head, and I was immediately unconscious. From accounts told by my friends, the damage was so bad on the car that my door was sitting inside of the passenger seat, I had to have my door cut off to be taken out of the car, and they secured my head and neck to take me onto the ambulance. What alarmed me about this is that I have absolutely no memory of anything that happened from the initial impact to actually being inside of the ambulance because I was unconscious.

    My friends have memories of me communicating with the officers and telling them where I was bleeding, telling them that I was going to be fine and that I was alive. I have no memory of this at all. From my perspective of it, I did not speak to any officers about my condition. I was not walking out of the car. I had a near death experience. I remember vividly seeing and hearing the people that I loved telling me that I had to wake up. I kept hearing "Wake up. Get up. Get up. Get up." I woke up briefly in the ambulance, confused to sirens, a smashed phone and my friend crying "Jas, I thought I killed you. I thought I killed you.", then nothing, until I heard a voice say: "Get up Jasmyn, It's not your time yet." I woke up fully conscious in the hospital room, alone. I had an IV connected to my arm, and all I can remember is my heavy breathing as I thought to myself trying to recall what had just happened.

    The third accident was in November. This was more minor simply because nobody was injured, but it was still highly traumatic. We were on our way home from a beautiful Thanksgiving break in Atlanta, visiting one of our other friend's family and the driver lost control of the car on the highway sending the car spinning about 6 times before stopping right before we hit the trees (I'm talking 1 foot away from the trees, y'all). We all hopped out of the car and looked at the highway. We were surprised that there were no cars near us on the road when we lost control over the car. I was in awe, because we were in one of the far-left lanes when this happened. As soon as we got out the car, we saw 4 large semi-trucks driving down the highway at full speed where we had just lost control of the car. Just then, I realized that if this would've happened any second later we would have all been seriously injured or even dead. I immediately dropped down, tears running down my face and said "God, there is no way other than by You that I keep getting in these accidents that I am supposed to die or be seriously injured in, and I keep making it our alive. Why do you keep saving me? Why do you need me to be here?", and just like that it all made sense.

    All of the moments of confusion and doubt that I was experiencing with my identity was answered in a prayer I made to God: *He needs me to be here.* God was trying to prove to me that He needed me to be here on this earth, in this life because I had a purpose. I was at a point in my life where I had no idea. I felt like I couldn't hear God when I called on Him. Everything was blurry, and everything that I thought was supposed to happen wasn't happening the way I thought it would. The confusion that I was feeling was causing me to run away from what I knew God wanted for me. The confusion prevented me from using my gifts and living in my purpose.

    I looked around and I saw all the people who didn't have good intentions or good motives getting ahead in life, and it made me think that I was doing something wrong. I had no clue what direction to go in. It felt like I had a blindfold on and I had no choice but to follow the voice of God, but where was His voice? God was trying to get my attention. He was trying to show me that through all of my fear, worry and confusion He is in control. At the time of the accidents, I thought that I was being punished. I was so upset because of the stress that I was under and the stress that I was putting on my family and I genuinely felt like I was bad luck.

I was in and out of the hospital for check-ups. Visiting to get stiches and staples removed, piling up hospital bills, seeing an attorney, seeing a neurologist, and so many other things that were pulling me from all angles. I ended not being able to attend school in the spring semester because of the hefty hospital bills. So, I had two options. First option, I could go home and hope for the best—which if what my family wanted me to do. Second option, I could stay and have faith that things would get better. I decided to stay. It was stressful, and the anxiety that I was feeling was overwhelmingly present as a result. I could barely eat, I lost a lot of weight, and I was constantly in a place of feeling lost. While everyone else was in school, I was looking for a job, and I honestly felt so stuck. It's as if life was going on without me.

Everything that I'd ever dealt with in my life caught up to me, but God was helping me to reclaim my time. He had to get my attention and adjust the focus back on Him. I started attending therapy again, and I was diagnosed with slight post-traumatic stress disorder (PTSD) from the accidents. My sessions at the FAMU Counseling Services office started to help me unravel the pain from within me. I began to heal from all the things that were holding me back. With consistent efforts and progress, I started to do the things I loved again. But, this time, I was truly happy while doing them. I would take walks by myself and explore the world around me. I'd sit at the park and read my bible or write in my journal. I was happy again. Eventually, I got the balance cleared from my account and I met with a new advisor that enrolled me into a few summer classes a week before they started.

Looking back, these accidents are what caused me to move closer spiritually to God. They made me start praying and asking questions more, they made me start writing more, they made me start reading the Bible more. I was on the path back to peace, guidance and myself. So, prayer and church became my life. I began to find solace and peace in nature. So, I would just sit outside and cry, I would sit outside and pray, and I would sit outside and write. On this journey into becoming the woman God put me here to be, I experienced different emotions. There's fear, there's pain, there's forgiveness, there's restoration, there's understanding, and there's so much more that we all experience in this life. I am growing so much, and it's a part of my purpose to share these things with others to help them along the way in their own journey.

Now the journey to becoming isn't always easy and it is sometimes scary because we can't see the outcome but that's what faith in action is – following God without exactly knowing where He's going to lead you and trusting that although the journey may be rocky, where you're headed is worth all that it encompasses. So, as you're starting your journey, or continuing your journey, I hope that my experiences will motivate and empower you to keep going to reach your destiny. And to all of you who know how it feels to want to have it all together I tell you as a reminder that it's okay to get down, just remember to get back up.

xo

A LETTER OF ENCOURAGEMENT

We all experience bad days that sometimes seem like the end of the world. Use this space to write a letter to your future self, letting him/her know that it's going to be alright because it is going to be alright.
(Remember to put the date on it!)

A LETTER ABOUT FEAR

2 Timothy 1:7 (KJV): For God has not given us a spirit of fear, but of power and of love and of a sound mind.

Fear is the one thing that can cripple and disable us from doing what we are called to do. It's something so strong that it can literally stop us from getting to where we are trying to go. In life, it keeps us still. In the midst of our decision making, it keeps us from moving in any direction. Fear cripples us. So, why do some of us get comfortable in fear? We use fear to keep safe. We use fear to keep us protected, but we also use fear to keep us in our comfort zone. Why does getting accepted into that school seem so impossible? Fear. Why does being successful and having the career you desire seem out of your reach? Fear. Why do you push away people that come close to getting to know the real you? Fear. Why can't you write the book? Fear. Why can't you start your business? Fear. Why can't you promote yourself when no one else supports you but yourself? Fear. The fear of being unnoticed, unaccepted, unappreciated, unsuccessful, and failing. But, what is fear actually doing? It's keeping you from trying. It's keeping from doing. It's keeping you from receiving the blessings. There cannot be faith and fear in the same spirit.

We are never alone in this life no matter how lonely we feel. The feelings of anxiety, fear, and doubt that keeps us away from the things that we want most in life will not have power over us if we decide to move through them. This means that although we may be fearful of what's to come, we will choose to continue moving anyway. Although we are nervous about starting this business, we're going to brainstorm and create a business plan anyway. Although this university only accepts 20-25 students into their program, we're going to apply anyway. Although, we're the only one who sees our vision and supports our vision, we're going to promote ourselves anyway. Although, we don't know if anyone is going to want to listen to what we have to say, we are going to put our knowledge into the world anyway.

In fear, there may be pressure in your spirit causing you to want to move away from the blessings. It can make you want to hide from the world. It can make you feel like something is after you but that is exactly what it's trying to do. Fear doesn't want you to be successful. Fear doesn't want you to realize your full potential. Fear wants to keep you stuck in the same place with the same mindset that's telling you that you "can't". So, how do we move through fear?

Well here's the first step, make a list of everything that scares you and write why it scares you. Then, write down what the fear is keeping you from. Is it keeping you from success? From happiness? From adventure? From love? How is the fear adding substance to your life? Are you going to continue to allow it to keep you away from the life you're desperately trying to live? The choice is yours. Make the decision today.

xo

A LETTER ABOUT PAIN

James 1:2-4 (NIV): Consider it pure joy, my brothers and sisters, whenever you face trials of many kinds, because you know that the testing of your faith produces perseverance. Let perseverance finish its work so that you may be mature and complete, not lacking anything.

Growing up, I never expected pain to be a part of the growth process. When we look at other people's success, we only see the glamorous side of growth. We don't see the crying, the hurting or the days where people want to quit. We see the outcome of the growth, and in truth it blinds us. We begin to think that things will come easy, and that the journey to living in our purpose will be all sunshine and no rain. Because other people have something, we think that we're supposed to have it, too. So, we begin to rush ourselves and try to escape the process as if we don't have to go through it anyway. We delay growth by avoiding the pain within the process of growth. Instead of running from it, we can allow ourselves to let it push us further into purpose. We can allow it to lead us closer to God into healing, and we can allow it to cultivate a beautiful perspective of the strength and the love that we have within ourselves.

Pain had a way of showing me how strong I was and how much

love I had inside of me. When I felt pain, I usually tried to run from it because I don't like feeling pain. I mean, who does? It's not fun, it's definitely not comfortable, and it hurts. So, why would I want to stay in a place where there is pain? I can remember times when I would do everything but acknowledge how I felt, but avoiding the pain only made it worse. I've tried to sleep it away or keep myself super busy so that I wouldn't feel it and I could pretend that it was gone, but in reality, it was still there.

Pain would make me feel alone, and when I felt alone I tended to push people away because I didn't feel like people were there for me the way I was there for them, and the truth is some of them weren't. I was not angry at these people because I understand that everyone is fighting their own individual battles and may not have had the strength to be there for me, but it truly hurt me. I felt lonely in a room full of people that knew me, but I felt like they didn't know me. I kept reminding myself through these times that God needed me to be strong, but I didn't want to be strong.

I found myself questioning why certain things were happening to me. I would say I'm a good person, my intentions are pure, I'm doing all the right things so why are these things happening to me? Why do I have to go through these things, and then fake being happy for everyone else's sake? I would be mad at God for making me sensitive, and for giving me this loving and nurturing spirit. I would be mad that I had to be the strong one, the mediator, and the level head. I didn't want to be that anymore, I wanted someone to be that for me. I was sick of being the strong person for everyone and then also having to come home, fight my own personal battles and be the strong person for myself too.

The truth is, pain is a very necessary, unavoidable part of life, and the purpose. Let me be clear and state that I am in no way saying that you must stay in an environment where you are being physically, emotionally or verbally abused, or disrespected. What I'm saying is that there are going to be some seasons where it feels like nothing is getting better and all of your efforts are being blocked or are going unnoticed. You're going to want to give up and you may even feel like there is no way possible that things will get better. There are going to be moments when God is calling you to do things, and when you do them it seems like nothing happens. But what we must understand, and what I still have to talk myself into at times, is that God is strategic. So even if it feels like He isn't there, He is. Even when it feels like He isn't working, He is and it's always for your good.

    I remember something that I heard once, that really stuck with me, and it goes: "We don't question the sun when it rises and sets. Even when we can't see the sun, we know that the darkness will soon be greeted with light." The same thing goes for God. Even though we can't see him, He's always working. Even in the darkest moments of our lives, we know that the Light will soon come to greet darkness. We can count on that.

    When we make the decision to keep going and not remain stuck we will start to see the things God is doing in our lives. Maybe He needs you in the place that you're in to teach you how to talk to Him. Maybe He allowed you to feel the pain, so that you could learn how to be strong without anyone else holding you together. Maybe He is trying to teach you that He is the glue for your brokenness. He may be pulling you away from things so that He can teach you something, but the thing about God is that He always restores, and He always comes through. So, prepare yourself for the blessing that is on the way.

xo

EXPERIENCING THE PAIN

USE THE SPACE BELOW TO WRITE ABOUT WHAT IS BRINGING YOU PAIN IN THIS SEASON, INCLUDE THIS PAGE IN YOUR NEXT PRAYER AND ASK FOR HEALING OVER THESE THINGS:

I CAN DEFINE MYSELF
By not allowing others to limit me
By not allowing others to force their realities on my healing
By healing in the most beautiful, expressive, open, honest and unapologetic way possible.
By telling the world who I am
And not allowing the world to make me who it wants me to be
I am not normal
I am extraordinary
I am ethereal
I am beauty
I am intelligence
I am knowledge
I am love
I am healing –
           personified.

Defining yourself takes power away from other people and puts it into your own hands. In what ways can you define yourself?

I.

Creation
flows from love.
The one true love that is
Perfect
in all of its ways.
The one that pours out from
selflessness and generosity.
Love
promotes creation.
It encourages growth in all aspects of life.
Flowers bloom with love.
Our love allows babies to grow
physically,
spiritually,
emotionally.
When we feed our souls,
we create spaces for ourselves to grow.
God so loved the world,
that He created it
and gave us His son
so that we may
experience
love.

II.

We are still beautiful
underneath
all of the pain
and madness.
There is still light within us.
I choose
to see the light instead of the darkness
so that I may stand
and receive
what God has for me.
We are
a beautiful creation
growing
in our consistent efforts.

III.

I'm always curious about humanity. Everyone sees the world from their own extremely unique perspectives – no one's world is exactly the same as someone else's. It's easier for me to accept people that way. What one person sees as strange, the other may see as beautiful. We don't appreciate each other's differences the way we should. We shame "different", when "different" can be beautiful. I find beauty in the oddest places. I appreciate the beauty in our differences—we all have qualities that we can learn from. So, teach me how to show the world that we were made this way.

– WE ARE ALIKE IN OUR DIFFERENCES

IV.

The guilt of the mistakes that you've made in the past and
the fear that you will make them again will never have
the power to hold you back if you understand that it's
behind you. Everyday you're getting better, healing, and growing.

V.

Sometimes you lose sight of how strong and whole you are –
    all by yourself.

    Your past tries to get a hold of you, and,
        Sometimes,
            you give in.

                But, you're stronger than you think.

VI.

In order for me to become
who I'm going to be in my destiny, I must
let go of who I am and who I was,
be open to growth and
surrender
my
need
to
control.

VII.

As a
Black Woman
I'm constantly put in a
box
of how people want me to be.
Being told that
I'm too loud.
I'm too quiet.
I love too hard.
I don't love at all.
When I'm passionate –
I'm angry.
When I'm upset –
I'm emotional.
I'm too thin.
I'm too fat.
Too nice.
A bitch.
Too open.
Too guarded.
So many things when
all I want to be
is a black woman
defined by me.

VIII.

Love liberates, so
why is being loved something to be afraid of?
Freedom.
Freedom.
Freedom.
Love
sets you free from yourself
and all of the things stopping you from
being.
See,
love shows you —
reveals to you
your truest self.
Love
breathes life into your soul.
Love
consumes fear.
Love
destroys fear
but we are so fearful of it.
We are in bondage
comfortably, but
can we heal there?
Or should we allow love
to free,
comfort
and heal
us

IX.

I am the only person who can define me.
I am on a constant journey of growth.
And I won't apologize if
the process
is not as beautiful as you expected
because it is.

X.

Let my voice
Change
Humanity —
and all of the things that dwell in the earth.
I want to be
Your vessel of love
and of light like
the Son,
that rose to bring light to dark places
and shines bright through the clouds and the rain.
and makes the flowers bloom
and the trees stand tall.
The one that gives us beauty in our skin,
and
brings warmth
into our coldness.
The one that nourishes us with
pure light.

Let my voice
be
a force so strong
that when I speak
they hear me.
I want to be
Your vessel of healing
like the Spirit
that healed
and lives
in me.

THE UNDERSTANDING

What does faith mean in your life? Many times, we can claim to live a faith filled life, but our minds are clouded with doubt. If we do not live out our faith it has no purpose. We claim to have faith, but we doubt, we don't trust God, we walk by sight. So, what does our faith really do for us? We're human, so I'm not bashing you because I do it too, but we have to learn collectively that faith without works is dead. Faith is believing in what God has for you even when you can't see how it's going to work out.

I've been through multiple occasions where I felt hopeless and my faith was shaken, and I had to rely on praying and asking for direction to get me through. One quality that I possessed from this is joy. Joy allows you to be creative. It allows you to create spaces to be vulnerable in and have faith while it hurts. Joy rejects bitterness and allows blessings to flow. It opens your heart to the blessings that are coming to you. I've learned that joy is a quality worth having. It's easier to see life through a positive lens when you're joyful. It's different than happiness because happiness comes and goes, but joy is found in your spirit. You are more resilient when you have joy. You are more hopeful when you have joy. You are stronger when you have joy because no one can take it from you and you know to expect blessings after the pain.

There are moments in our life when we feel weakened by all of the things going on. This is the time that God is able to prove himself through the storm. He loves when we get to places where we feel stuck, weak or like there's no way that we will get better because that's when we come to Him, and it's His moment to shine and prove to us that He has us covered. God wants us to live a life that we love, and a life that we are happy in. Do you believe that?

A LETTER ABOUT PEACE

Philippians 4:7 (NIV): And the peace of God, which transcends all understanding, will guard your hearts and your minds in Christ Jesus.

Forgiving yourself is vital in order to have a healthy relationship with yourself. Think about how big of a role forgiveness plays in your everyday life: friends, partners, family, and with God. When we hold back from forgiveness, we can see changes in our behavior from ourselves towards other people. We may start to distance ourselves, not want to speak to them or we could even end the friendship all together, but what happens when we don't forgive ourselves? You can't cut your relationship off with yourself, so what do you do? Withholding forgiveness from yourself leads to extreme self-criticism, low self-esteem and feelings of worthlessness, anger and resentment towards yourself. Why? Because you're mad at yourself for making a mistake, and you won't apologize to yourself and forgive yourself.

So many times, we are held back by the repetitive subconscious reminders of our mistakes, disappointments and failures. Our minds hold us captive to the thought that we won't be able to move past this mistake, or when we go to try a different route we believe that the same thing is going to happen. So, all of these reminders of our faults and flaws force us into perfection. We start to think that we have to have it all together to be worthy. We start to compare where we are in our journey to where other people are in their journey. RED FLAG! We make mistakes because we are not made to be perfect. We are human, and there is no way that any of us can be perfect, and the good news is, we don't have to be. Our goal is not to aim for perfection, but for growth.

I am still in a place of learning and growing just like those of you reading this book and I want to always be in that place. I pray to always be in a place that I can be open to changing and learning things outside of myself. I want to always be in a place of growth, so that I'm always finding new ways to impact this world – and I wish the same for you.

I am growing into a place of understanding that trials come to make us stronger. I'm understanding that my tears don't make me weak. It is easy to feel like our tears bring weakness, but tears show strength. When you've been being strong for yourself, your body will let you know that it's okay to feel. Your body will let you know that it's okay to release those feelings. So, don't let the tears make you stop because that's the wrong answer. Continue to push through even while they are falling because you are a warrior, and you can get through this.

Don't be convinced by the circumstances that what you're dealing with is a punishment. There is no trial that you will face that will have the strength to break you, although it will try. These things that come your way that seem like mountains will teach you how to climb. These things that come your way that seem like walls will teach you how to break through them. God lets us go through these things to gain a better understanding of His character. He fights your battles, and leaves you wondering how you got through it.

God wants us to cling to His promises and His word trusting that He is working on our behalf. He is going to do exactly what He said He would do. So, it is important that we do not attempt to rush through these trials because they take place for us to bloom into completeness. Sometimes we are so focused on what's going wrong that we close our eyes to the things that God is already doing in our lives. All of our life, God proves that we can trust Him, and when we doubt His abilities, we are proving that God cannot trust us.

We prove ourselves trustworthy to God by allowing ourselves to trust Him with our whole hearts, not wavering because He keeps His promises. In order for us to walk in our blessings, we must not block them with our doubts. He uses these times to make us stronger and to help us grow into the person who we are supposed to be. The person who does not run away under the pressures of trials but endures them and trusts God through them will receive all that God has for them. So, what does God have for you? Will you trust Him?

EXTENDING FORGIVENESS

We always hear about the importance of forgiving others, but it's also important that we forgive ourselves.

Make a list of things that you've been beating yourself up about or replaying in your mind:

_____
_____
_____
_____
_____
_____
_____
_____
_____
_____
_____
_____
_____
_____
_____
_____
_____
_____
_____
_____
_____
_____
_____
_____
_____
_____
_____
_____

Now, take this list, go to the mirror and forgive yourself for these things. (Ex: I am upset with myself for dropping the pizza that I just ordered. I am a human that makes mistakes and has slippery fingers, but I forgive myself because I love myself and I am still worthy of living a life without regret.)

A LETTER ABOUT RESTORATION

Jeremiah 33:6 (NIV): **Nevertheless, I will bring health and healing to it; I will heal my people and will let them enjoy abundant peace and security.**

After all of the crying, hurting, and wondering, there will come peace. The peace of knowing that you are protected, and that nothing can destroy what God has for you. The peace in knowing who you are and standing firm in your truth. The peace that you feel in your heart and your spirit where there is no fear, no anger, and no doubt. The peace in knowing that there is no way a promise that God made to you can be changed. The peace in knowing who you are and standing firm in your truth. The peace in knowing that you don't have it all together, but you are a work in progress, and you are on the way to greatness.

You will look back and see that you have grown to a place where you are focused in purpose. A place where all of the noise is silenced, and you are allowed to grow into the person that God wants you to become. You will feel peace within your mind because you will have power over the thoughts that once haunted you and caused you to run in fear. You will feel peace in your spirit because you will know that what God has for you is for you, and that He is guiding your steps. You will have peace in knowing that you don't need to prove yourself to anyone who has the wrong idea of you because it doesn't matter how other people perceive you. Start giving yourself the space to be yourself, and to grow. It wasn't until I learned how to say "no" and allowed myself the space to grow as a woman that I became my happiest self and grew confident in the person that I knew I was.

Take the time to understand that yes, other people need you, but you need you too. You cannot continue to allow yourself to be drained by helping and giving to others without loving yourself back to fullness. That "draining" feeling comes from giving pieces of your heart to give others encouragement, love, hope, support and so many other things, but it's important to give yourself time to allow God's love to piece your heart back together when you feel like the weight of your life's purpose is too heavy on your spirit. No matter how much love you give out, you are always able to put that love back inside of yourself.

God knows each of us personally. He knows our hearts, minds and spirits. He knows our personalities, what we like and don't like. He knows all of these things about us, so we don't need to search on earth for the things that we already have in Him. He loves us in perfection, no matter what we do, no matter how our pasts were, and no matter how lost we feel. There is such beauty found in that kind of love. When people speak negatively about you, know that God has your back. When people pray against your gifts and future with false motives and negative thoughts about your life, know that God has your back. No weapon – physical, verbal, emotional or mental – has ever had the power to harm you because He loves you. You will begin to see your growth, feel your growth and truly see that joy comes after all of this.

As I look back over the things that I've experienced, I understood that all of it had to happen. The good, the bad, the beautiful and the ugly all assisted in my growing. Once seasons of pain end, God allows His blessings to flow because you are prepared to receive them. We can't accept new blessings or opportunities without a changed mind or attitude. It's all about preparation. You're growing during those times, whether you choose to acknowledge it or not. He was preparing you in the pain just like He was preparing me in the pain.

We deserve peace, happiness and love. We deserve joy. We deserve success. We all deserve a life that we love, despite what our past was like, despite where we come from, despite family history, despite what we did the other day.

We are the chosen ones. We are the ones who have to break the cycles. We are the ones who have to work hard to change ourselves, so our children won't have to go through the things that we went through. We have to make differences in our environment so that the people that come after us can live peacefully. We have to decide that the devil cannot have our futures. He's had his hand on too much of our pasts, but even the devil knows God is in control. What God blesses, no man can curse, separate or destroy and He has touched every aspect of your life with blessings.

So, don't desire to live in someone else's life because you have no idea what it took for them to get there. They are fighting their own battles that you probably couldn't even handle. You are fighting your own battles that they probably couldn't even handle, but the good news is your battles are yours and theirs are theirs. Your journey is unique to what you are called to do on this Earth, and in this life. God has you exactly where He needs you in every moment of your life.

Although it may hurt at times, life doesn't always feel the way we want it to feel but we can learn to appreciate life through the good times and the bad times. So, choose to be patient. Choose to be still. Choose to be confident. Choose to be hopeful. Choose to remain joyful. Choose to live in your truth. Most importantly, choose to keep going with the faith that God is going to lead you to where you need to be.

With love,
Jasmyn Ruja

NOTE TO SELF

Made in the USA
San Bernardino, CA
11 June 2018